FELIX THE FOX AND HIS FIERY TEMPER

WRITTEN BY
LINDSEY COKER HARRIS

ILLUSTRATED BY
TANYA MATIIKIV

Copyright © 2023 Lindsey Coker Harris

All rights reserved.

ISBN: 978-1-7358803-5-8

Felix the Fox was a mostly cheerful fox.
But when he got angry, you could definitely tell.

Felix would scream
and he would shout.

Felix would cry
and he would roar.

When Mommy told him he had to stop playing and come downstairs for dinner, he smashed some of his toys.

When Daddy told him it was time for school, he broke his new video game console.

When Granny said he had to eat his vegetables, he threw his plate on the floor.

When Grandpa asked him to get ready to go out, he ripped his favorite shirt.

As soon as Felix felt angry, he always wanted to **break** something.
Until one day, he realized he had destroyed all of his favorite things!

Now he had no favorite toys to play with.
He couldn't turn on his video game console.

He had to eat his dinner off a little plastic plate.
And he could no longer wear his favorite BLUE t-shirt.

When someone asked him to do something he didn't want to do, Felix would lash out.

But now he realized he was only hurting himself.

Letting his anger get the best of him was getting him nowhere.

Felix decided that he needed to find a new way to deal with his anger.

The next time Mommy asked him to come down for dinner, he took three deep breaths and remembered that it would be a tasty meal.

YUM

The next time Daddy told him to get ready for school, he thought about how he would get to see his best friends.

When Granny said to eat up his vegetables, Felix remembered that they would help him grow into a
big, strong fox.

And when Grandpa asked him to get ready to go out, he thought about what fun they would have together.

He realized that most of the time, there was no reason to feel angry at all!
Felix even found a new hobby that helped to calm him down during his angry moments...

FIXING THINGS!

He fixed his favorite toy with some thread.

He fixed his video game console with some screws.
He fixed his dinner plate with some glue and tape.

And with Daddy's help, he fixed his favorite shirt on the sewing machine.

Fixing things was so much fun! And it made Felix feel calm and relaxed.

From that day on, Felix rarely ever got angry.

He reminded himself that anger only leads to bad things. He would much rather control that anger and avoid the bad things altogether.

Felix the fox used to be known for his fiery temper.
Now Felix the fox is known for his

FRIENDLY FACE!